Dee Dee Wi

You May Now Kiss the Dog!

And Other Verbal Slip-ups

AUSTIN MACAULEY PUBLISHERS™

LONDON • CAMBRIDGE • NEW YORK • SHARJAH

Foreword

I first suspected that life with Dee Dee would be far from normal when, on our first date, she offered her 'compliments to the shelf' as we left a restaurant in central London.

We know from 'A Hard Day's Night' and 'Tomorrow Never Knows' – Ringo's phrases utilised as album and song titles by the Fab Four – that the malapropism is an occurrence that never fails to create mirth and sometimes hilarity.

Dee Dee is a malapropist and never ceases to keep me on my toes as I attempt to understand what she is trying to say.

Welcome to the following pages which not only demonstrate an excellent and sometimes rather offensive use of the English language, but also display her unique and somewhat alarming illustrations.

May taste and political correctness never darken her door.

Henry Marsh

This book is dedicated to all those who suffer from Lapsus Linguae

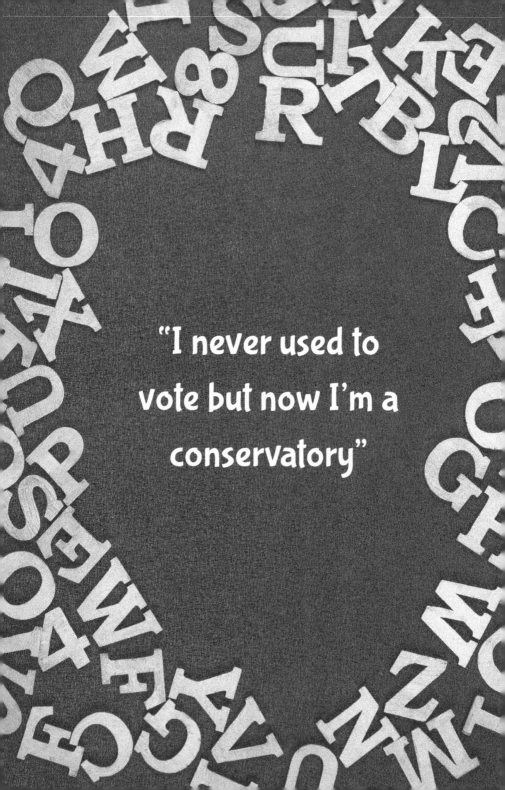

"I never used to vote but now I'm a conservatory"

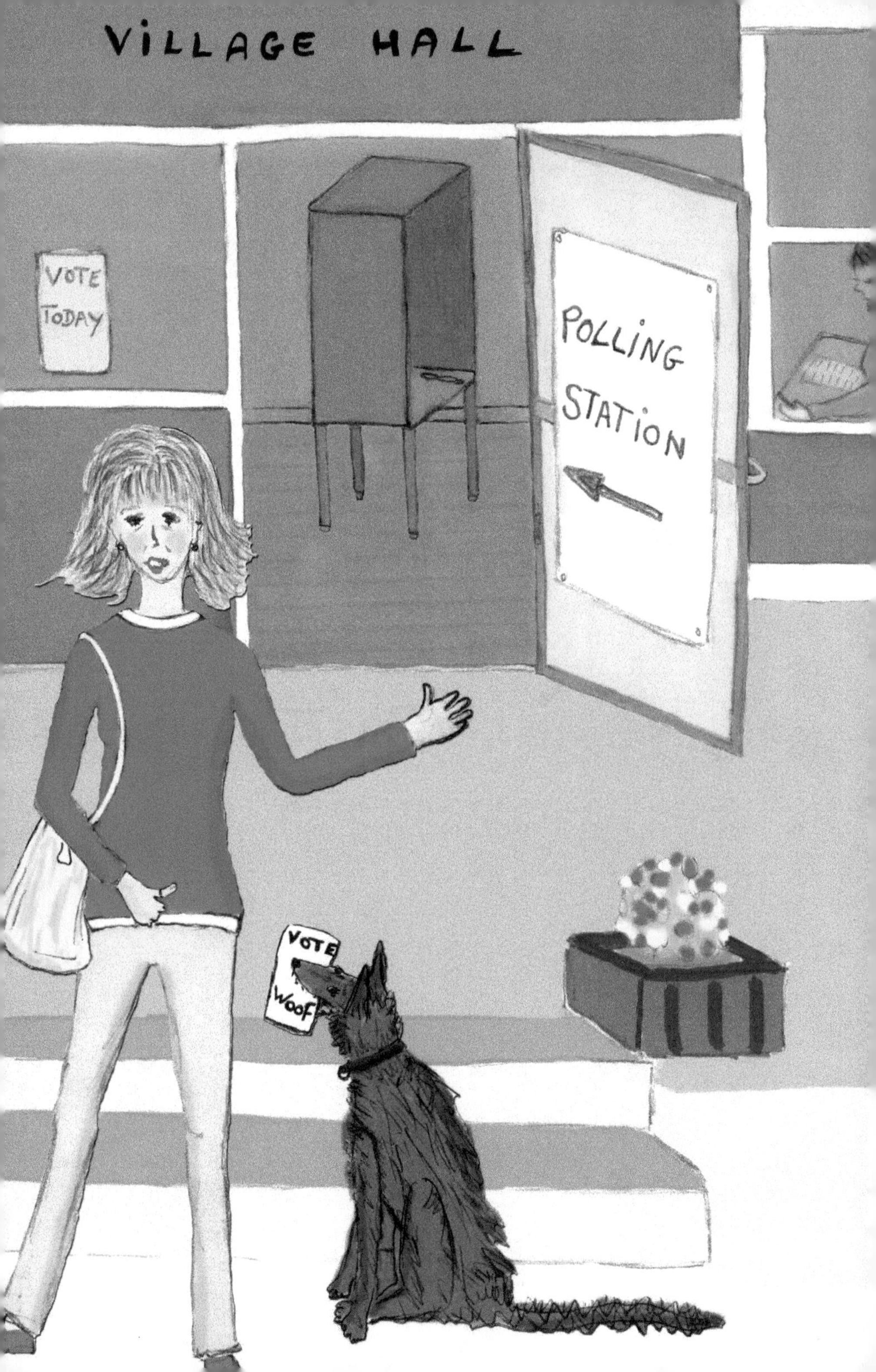
VILLAGE HALL
VOTE TODAY
POLLING STATION
VOTE
Woof

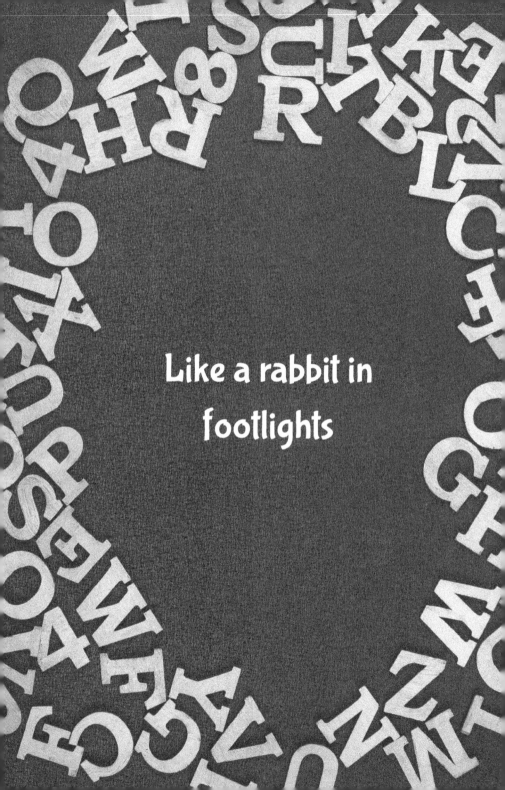

Like a rabbit in
footlights

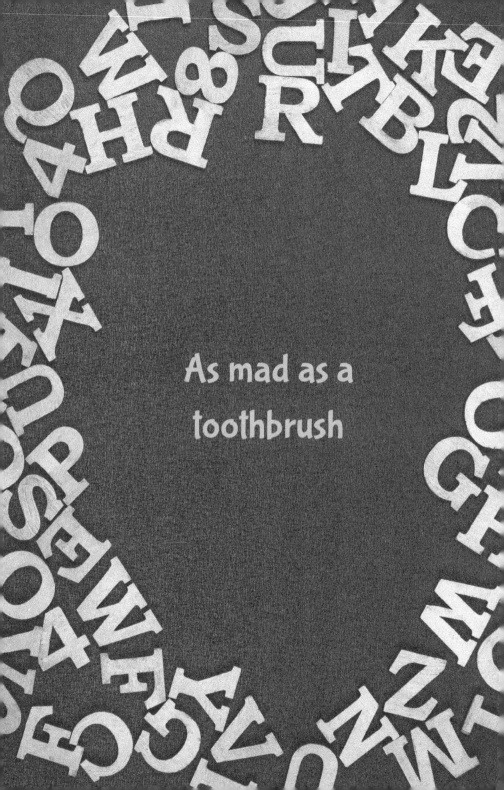

As mad as a
toothbrush

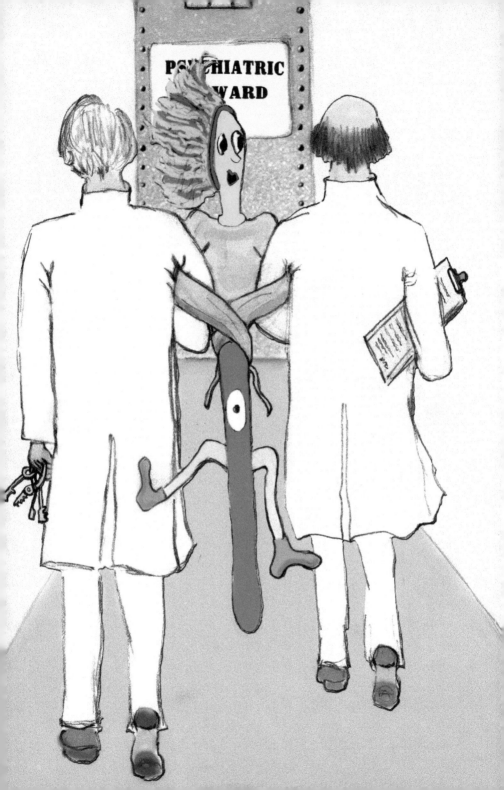

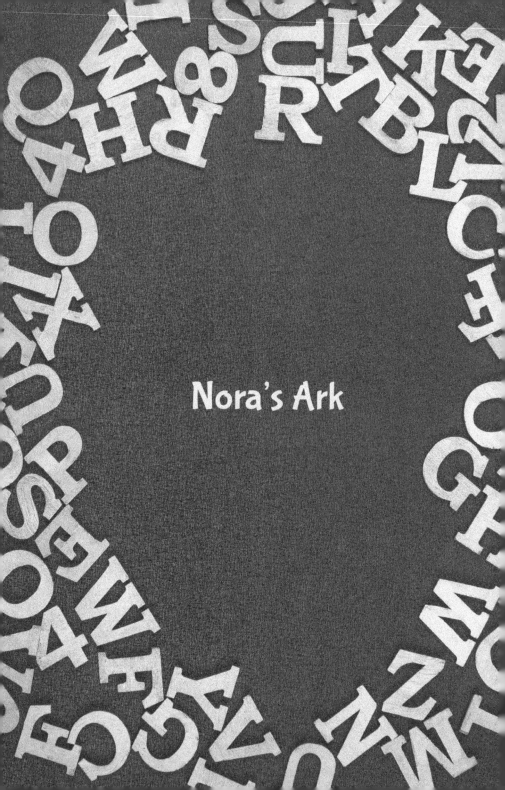

Nora's Ark

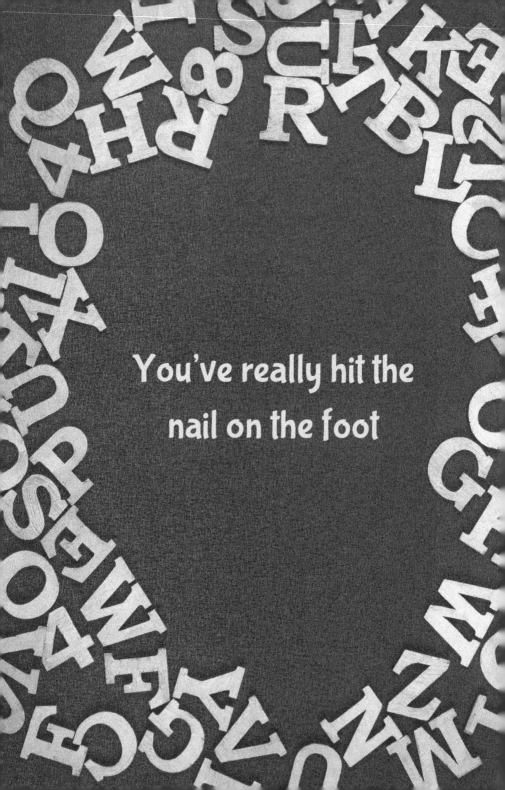

You've really hit the
nail on the foot

Hunting

shooting

and farting.

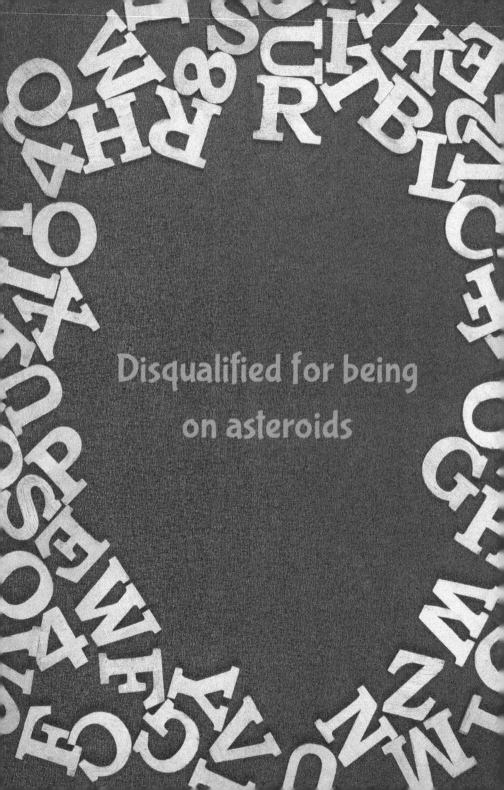

Disqualified for being

on asteroids

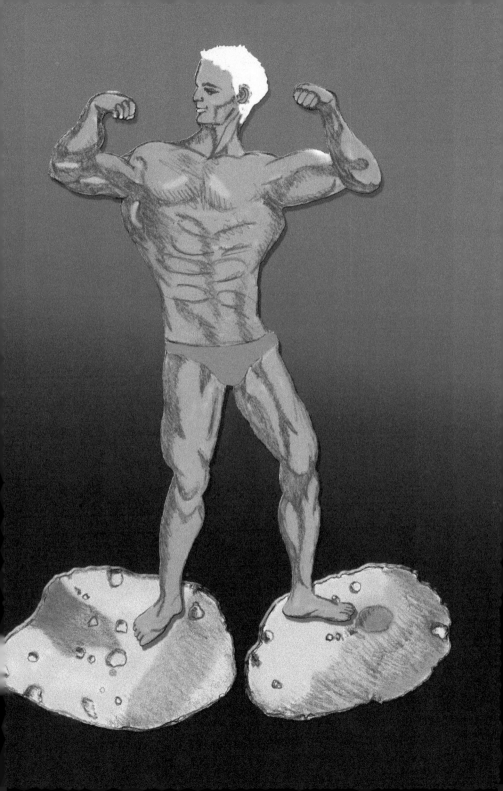

"They had to put a compost on his leg"

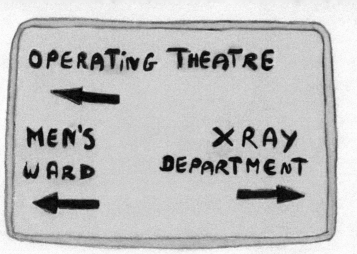

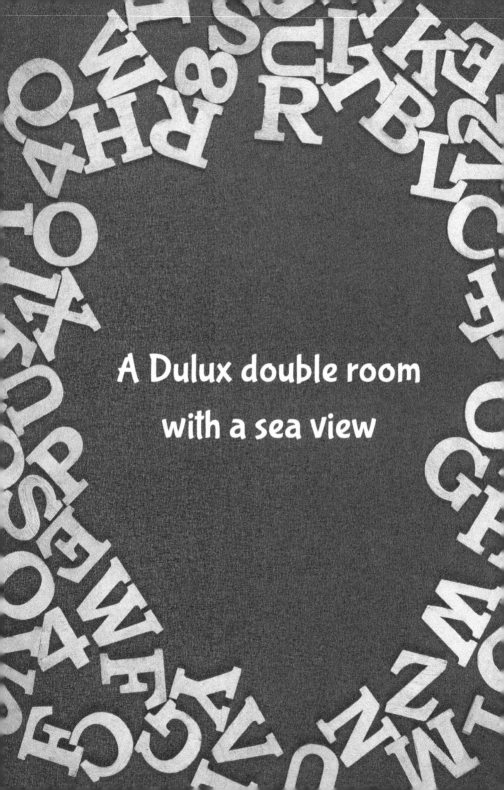

A Dulux double room
with a sea view

Two planks screw

of a loose

Killing two stones with one bird

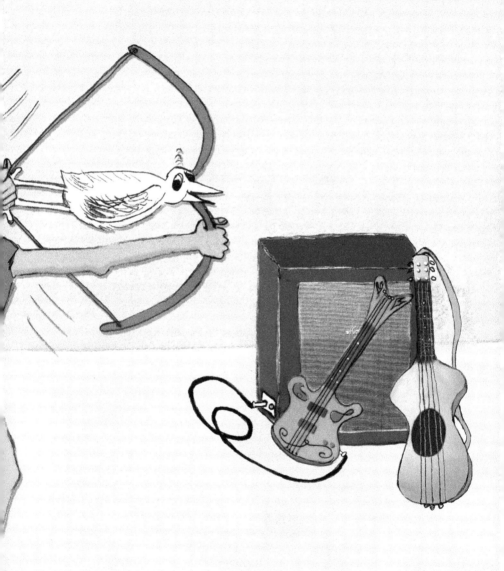

The Pied
Piper of
Hamlet

Exclamation mike!

"You should only get drugs on subscription"

It was very busy on the runaway

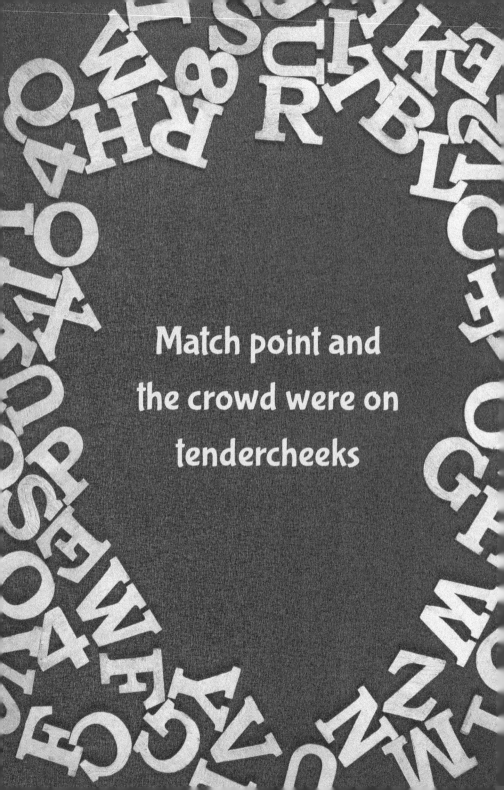

Match point and
the crowd were on
tendercheeks

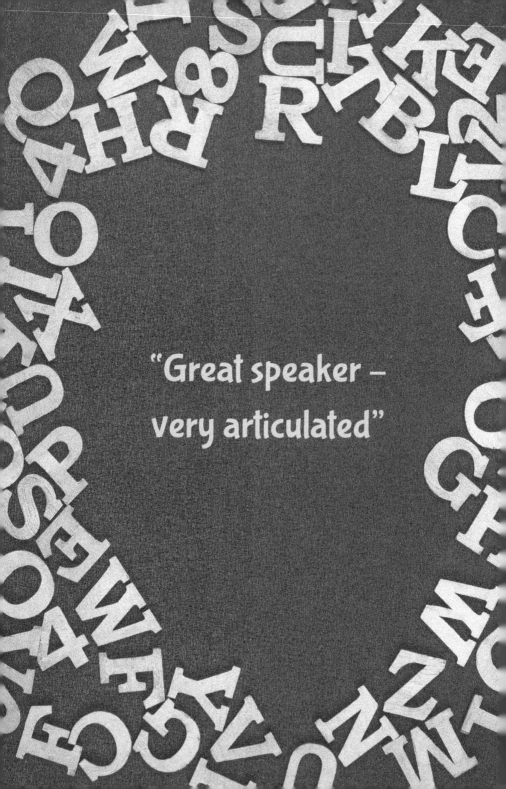

"Great speaker –
very articulated"

The manicurist gave
me an excellent
pedigree

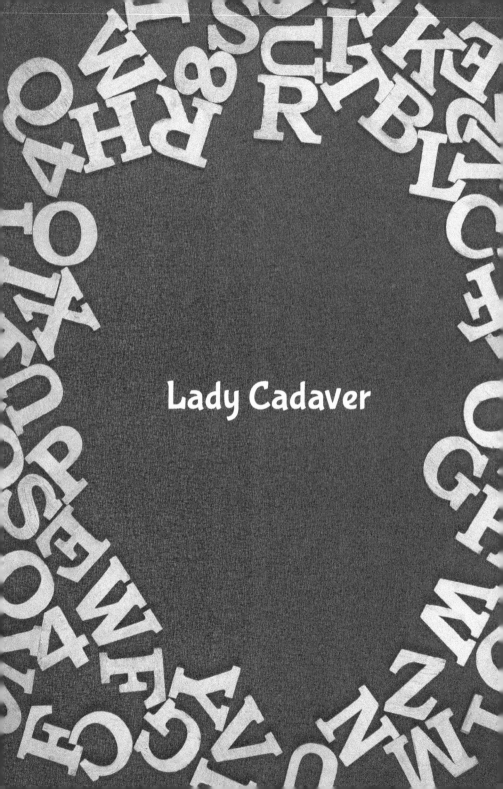

Lady Cadaver

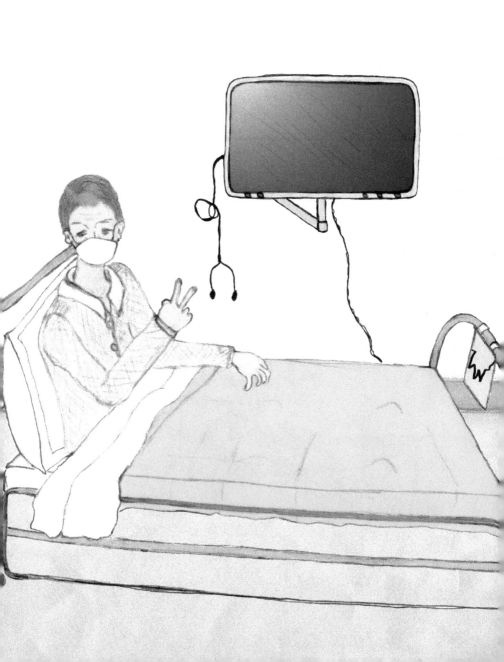

Gesticular cancer

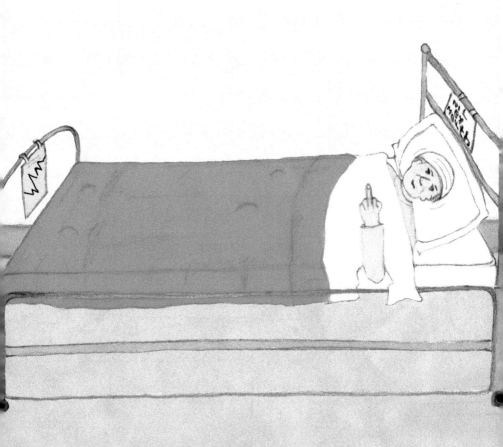

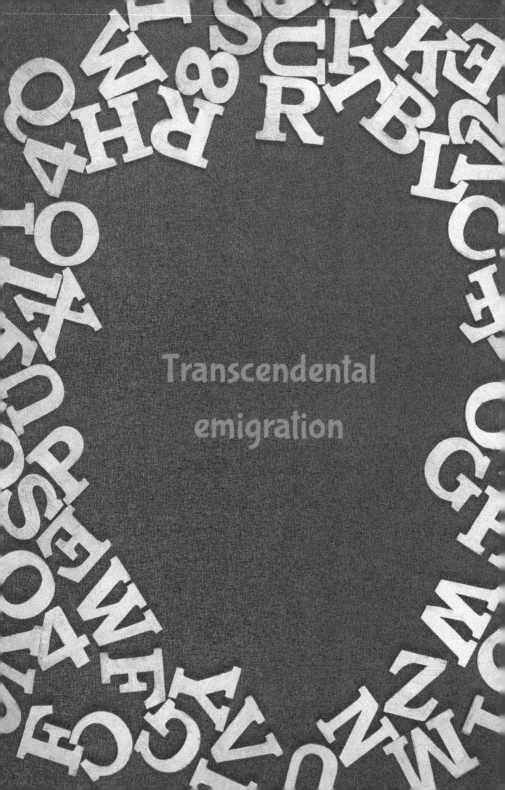

Transcendental emigration

There's always a carrot
at the end of the tunnel

He was arrested ar

marched off in cufflinks

We went up the

mountain in

a podcast

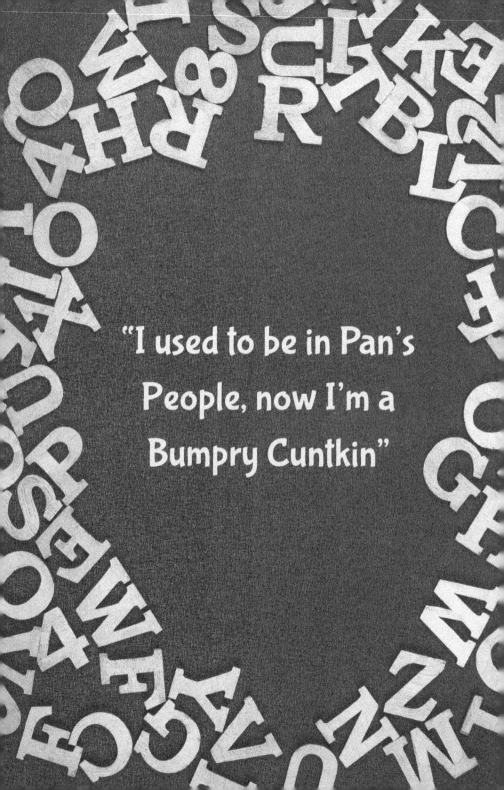

"I used to be in Pan's People, now I'm a Bumpry Cuntkin"

I would like to thank Henry Marsh for his never-ending support and patience in producing this book.

It has been a wonderful collaboration and I wouldn't have been able to get this together without his talent, skill and input.

Many of you know my eternal passion for dancing, but this is a new artistic release for me and I would like to share it with you.

This is my first attempt at drawing, but somehow I feel comfortable expressing my appalling misuse of the English language in – dare I say it? – art form!

I hope you had a chuckle and enjoyed my efforts as much as I enjoyed putting pencil to paper.

About the Author

Dee Dee lives in Wiltshire with her composer husband Henry Marsh and her two dogs Basil and Pickwick. Her inspiration for this book was their original, beloved German Shepherd dog, Uli.

She has two children from her previous marriage, Alexander and Poppy, and three stepchildren, Thomas, Oliver and Laura, plus Magnus, her first step-grandchild.

Dee Dee was a founder member of the famous '70s TV dance group Pan's People, who appeared on *Top of The Pops* every week for a decade. She still dances and teaches around the West Country and on line: www.deedeewilde.co.uk + Facebook.

This is her second book, the first being *Pan's People: Our Story*, which she co-wrote with the other members of the group.

A CIP catalogue record for this title is available from the British Library.

ISBN 9781528913607 (Paperback)
ISBN 9781528914697 (Epub e-Book)

www.austinmacauley.com

First Published (2020)
Austin Macauley Publishers Ltd
25 Canada Square
Canary Wharf
London
E14 5LQ

CPSIA information can be obtained
at www.ICGtesting.com
Printed in the USA
LVHW020925301220
675248LV00026B/879